For Linda,
a celebration.
B. P.

Text copyright © 1999 by Brian Patten
Illuminated letters, title page, cover artwork copyright ©1999 by Siân Bailey
A, B, C copyright © 1999 by David Armitage
D, G, V copyright © 1999 by Tim Clarey
E, N copyright © 1999 by Patrick Benson
F, I copyright © 1999 by David Parkins
H, M, R copyright © 1999 by Cathie Felstead
J, T, Z copyright © 1999 by Karin Littlewood
K, Q, W copyright © 1999 by Helen Ward
L, O copyright © 1999 by Jane Ray
P, S, X copyright © 1999 by Jason Cockcroft
U, Y copyright © 1999 by Nick Maland

Library of Congress Catalog Card # 99-70822
ISBN: 0-439-07969-1

10 9 8 7 6 5 4 3 2 1   0/0 1 2 3 4

Printed in China
First American edition, March 2000

THE BLUE & GREEN ARK

AN ALPHABET FOR PLANET EARTH

by

BRIAN PATTEN

with illustrations by

DAVID ARMITAGE, SIÂN BAILEY, PATRICK BENSON, TIM CLAREY,
JASON COCKCROFT, CATHIE FELSTEAD, KARIN LITTLEWOOD, NICK MALAND,
DAVID PARKINS, JANE RAY *and* HELEN WARD

SCHOLASTIC PRESS · NEW YORK

A is for Ark,

For the blue and green Ark adrift in the dark.

B is for Beginning, for the birth of all that surrounds
The blue and green Ark adrift in the dark.

C is for Cauldron,

For the earth's cooling core and the creation of all

On the blue and green Ark adrift in the dark.

D is for the Dinosaur and the Dodo,

Symbols of all that have long vanished

From the blue and green Ark adrift in the dark.

E is for the Eagle and its eyrie,

And for the eggs the eyrie shelters.

It is for the emerald and elderberry,

The emu and elephant.

It is for the eye that can see all things

On the blue and green Ark adrift in the dark.

F is for the Fire around which Neanderthal man crouched,

For the flames that kept at bay the saber-toothed tiger,

The perishing cold, the unknown demons.

It is for the flight of migrating birds and the frontiers beneath them,

For the fish, floating like golden submarines beneath lily-pads.

G is for the Gorilla snuggling down in its gigantic nest,

For the giraffe, tallest of living animals.

It is for the gold-dust and the gem, the greenfly and the gillyflower,

For the gleaming, phosphorescent glow-worm, alive with its own light.

H is for the Hawkmoth,
For the humming of its soft wings
As it hovers over flowers in the evening garden.
It is for the honeybee and the hive, for the honeybear,
And the horse champing grass in the wet fields.

I is for Icebergs,

For those massive, glittering bulks of ice

That creak and groan in the Arctic silence.

It is for the ice floes on which the cautious seal rests,

Where the polar bear wanders, sniffing out its prey.

It is for the pack ice that fits like a white skullcap on the head

Of the blue and green Ark adrift in the dark.

J is for Joy and for the scent of jasmine.
It is for the jaybird chattering in ecstasy,
For the juniper with its dark, purple berries,
For the taste of jelly beans,
For the best joke in the world.

K is for the Kingfisher flitting across rivers,

A blue sapphire made of feathers,

Its plumage so like the colors

Of the blue and green Ark adrift in the dark.

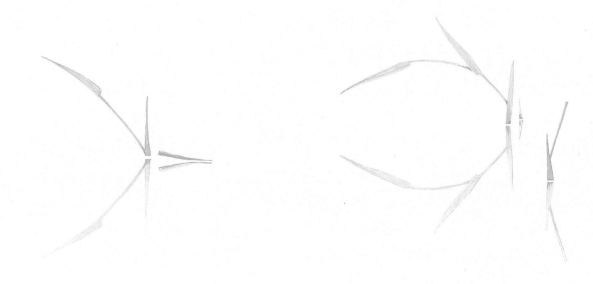

L is for Language.

For the language of the human tongue,

For the language of the lion's roar,

For the language of the bee's dance,

For the language made by the cricket's wings,

For the language of the beating heart

Heard by a child in the mother's womb.

It is for the languages of all things that communicate

On the blue and green Ark adrift in the dark.

M is for the Mammoth, buried for centuries
Beneath a wilderness of snow and ice.
It is for the mayfly that lives a single day,
For the marigold at summer's end –
A golden button ripped from summer's coat,
Glowing in the tired garden.

N is for the Narwhal.

Thrown up onto ancient shores, the skeleton of its twisted tusk

Gave birth to the legend of the unicorn.

It is for the nuzzle of the fox,

For the nose that sniffs out danger,

For the night and its shadows creeping

Across the blue and green Ark adrift in the dark.

O is for Ocean,

For the single ocean that covers the earth.

Hardly able to comprehend its immensity,

We split it into sections and give it different names,

Its depths less known to us than the moon.

P is for the Planets –

For the planet Mars, with its red desert,

Its canyons and melting permafrost,

For the planet Venus, with its vast clouds of sulphuric acid,

For the planet Mercury, formed by the Sun's debris,

For Pluto, a tiny ball of frozen gas on the edge of everything,

For giant Jupiter, with its storms that rage a thousand years,

For Saturn, so light in density it might float in water,

For remote Uranus, for Neptune –

Earth is so unique among them.

How much more precious then the tiniest poppy seed,

How awesome and God-like

The tiniest moth clinging to a blade of grass

On the blue and green Ark adrift in the dark.

Q is for the Quagga,

Half horse, half zebra,

A beautiful pony-sized creature

Hunted to extinction a few lifetimes ago.

And it is for the quelili,

The majestic brown hawk that followed it into oblivion,

Its fate the same. Now only its ghost hovers over

The blue and green Ark adrift in the dark.

R is for Rainforests.

Within them, from their dark green floors

To the tops of their cathedral-sized trees

Live half of all animal and plant species that exist

On the blue and green Ark adrift in the dark.

S is for the Stars that shiver and burn beyond the rim of the earth,
For the snowdrops drenched by spring rain,
For the nightingale's song, for the hissing snake,
For the moon-swollen seas, and the silence of underground caverns.

T is for Time,

For the twenty billion years that have melted and gone
Since our Solar System began.
It is for the thistledown blown by a child counting the hours.
It is for the tick of a watch.
It is for the tabby-cat and the tortoise
Asleep in the shade of the tulip tree.

U is for all the Utopias unattained,

For the unborn, uncurling like ferns in the womb,

For the umbilical cord linking us

To the blue and green Ark adrift in the dark.

V is for the Volcanoes that straddle the earth's broken crust.

It is for the vibrations that run along a spider's web,

For the vampire-bat hovering over the sleeping man,

Lapping blood as gently as a kitten laps milk.

W is for Winter,

And for the wolf trotting beneath icicles hanging like catkins

In the lonely, snow covered forest.

It is for the whale and its brethren,

With their half-ton hearts beating like giant drums,

With their songs that echo across all the oceans

Of the blue and green Ark adrift in the dark.

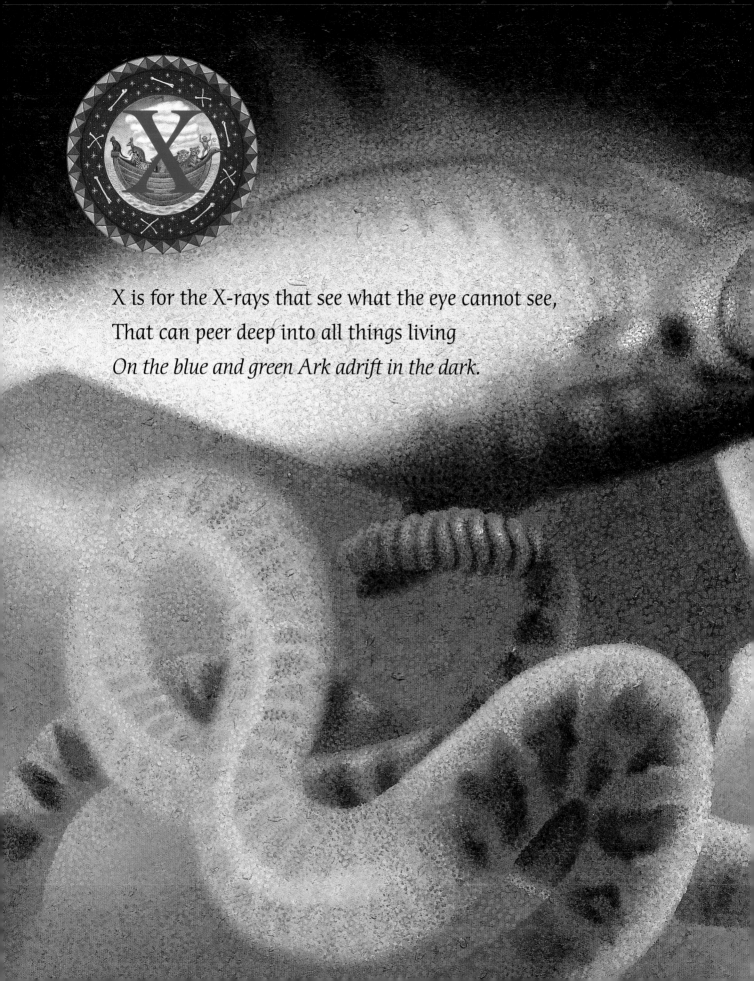

X is for the X-rays that see what the eye cannot see,

That can peer deep into all things living

On the blue and green Ark adrift in the dark.

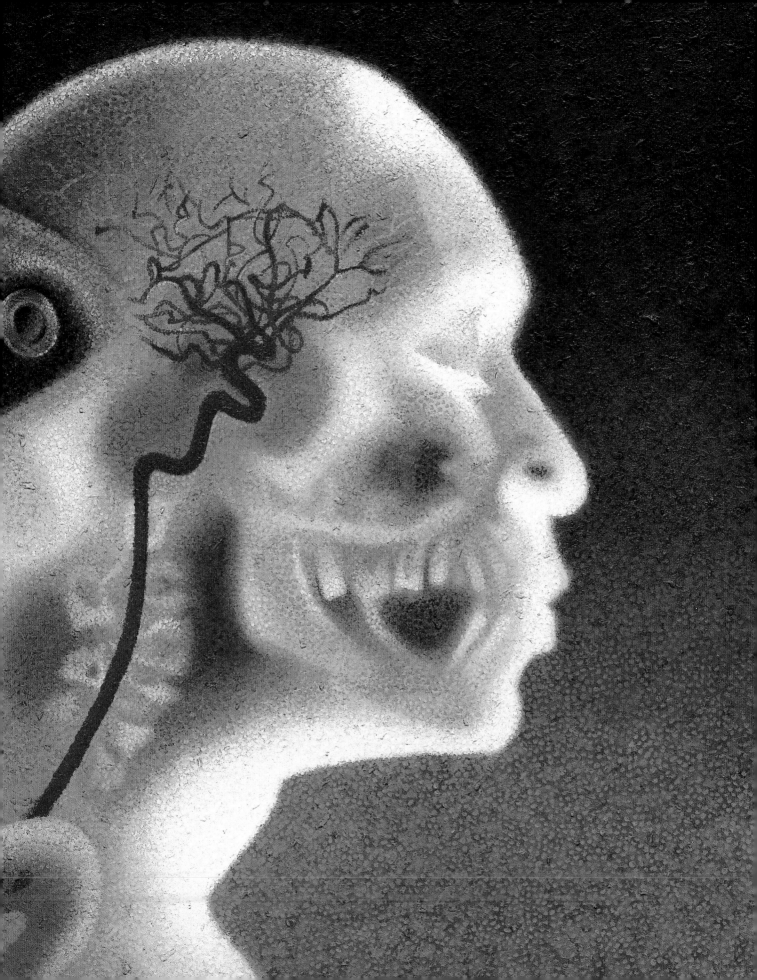

Y is for Yolk,

The yolk of an egg.

Yellow as the Sun, it nourishes all that the egg encloses

As the Sun's warmth nourishes all things

On the blue and green Ark adrift in the dark.

Z is for the Zodiac.

In that map of Heaven drawn with stars

We read our futures.

And it is for zero,

For the futures we will not have,

For the nothing we will become unless we cherish

The blue and green Ark adrift in the dark.

GLOSSARY

ILLUMINATED LETTERS BY SIÂN BAILEY, IN WATERCOLOR AND INK.
The following glossary covers just a few of the interesting or unusual things mentioned in the book. There are lots more things to spot if you look closely.

A ILLUSTRATED BY DAVID ARMITAGE IN WATERCOLOR AND MIXED-MEDIA.

Ammonite — An extinct seashell, from the time of dinosaurs, now commonly found as a fossil. Its closest modern relative is the wonderfully named Pearly Nautilus.

Ark — The original Ark was built by Noah. God told him to build it with windows and a door on each side. It had three decks, each divided into compartments. Noah was told to take into the Ark his family, plus one pair, a male and a female, of every beast, bird and reptile, with enough food for all of them.

B ILLUSTRATED BY DAVID ARMITAGE IN WATERCOLOR AND MIXED-MEDIA.

Breath — All land-living animals need to breathe to survive, taking in oxygen from the air and breathing out carbon dioxide. The balance of different gases in the air is changed by the effects of pollution and, if seriously affected, can become life-threatening for some animals, including humans.

C ILLUSTRATED BY DAVID ARMITAGE IN WATERCOLOR AND MIXED-MEDIA.

Creatures — There are over 40 million different kinds of living creatures on Earth.

D ILLUSTRATED BY TIM CLAREY IN WATERCOLOR.

Dawn — Every day that dawns, another three species of animal, bird, insect, or plant become extinct.

Diamonds — Exceptionally hard mineral, the hardest natural substance known. They are usually colorless, but are sometimes tinted by impurities, so diamonds can be yellow, orange, blue, brown, or black.

Dinosaur — Extinct terrestrial reptile, abundant in Mesozoic era. Dinosaurs lived on Earth for millions of years, finally becoming extinct approximately 65 million years ago. The remains of new kinds of dinosaurs are still being discovered today.

Dodo — A flightless bird extinct since the middle of the 17th century. Dodos were found in Mauritius and its surrounding islands. The dodo had a hooked bill, short, stout legs, and greyish plumage. They became extinct because of the introduction by settlers of dogs, pigs, and rats, which ate the dodos' eggs. They were also hunted and killed for sport and eaten by pirates — but by all accounts they were not very tasty.

Dove — The third bird to be sent by Noah from the Ark was another dove, which returned with an olive leaf in its beak. This was how Noah knew the flood was over.

Dragonfly — These predatory insects have large heads and eyes, long, slender bodies, and two pairs of irridescent wings, which they keep outspread when at rest. Dragonfly larvae are aquatic and can spend up to three years in water before emerging.

E ILLUSTRATED BY PATRICK BENSON IN INK LINE AND WATERCOLOR.

Eagle — America's eagles are the Golden Eagle and the Bald Eagle, the official emblem of the United States. These powerful birds of prey have large, broad wings.

Eggs — Almost every life-form on Earth starts as an egg — insects, fish, reptiles, birds, mammals.

Elements — In ancient and medieval times, people believed the universe was made up of just four elements: earth, air, fire and water.

Elephant — There are two main types of elephant, the larger African elephant, and the smaller, Indian elephant of South and Southeast Asia. The African elephant was declared an endangered animal in 1989, and ivory trading was banned, but poachers are still a threat to this huge mammal. The number of Asian elephants has been depleted through loss of their habitat, as their homeland is cultivated by people who need it for farming food.

Emerald — This gem is a green, transparent variety of beryl. After diamonds, the emerald is considered to be the most precious gem.

Emu — These large, Australian birds cannot fly and are similar to ostriches.

Eyrie — A nest on a cliff or mountaintop.

F ILLUSTRATED BY DAVID PARKINS IN GOUACHE.

Falcon — A bird of prey, typically with pointed wings and a long tail. They are often trained by people and have been used since Roman times to hunt small game.

Flamingo — These large wading birds have pink or red plumage and downwards bent bills. They live in slightly briny or salty lakes. They are found in many places, including Africa, Asia, Europe, South America and the Caribbean.

G ILLUSTRATED BY TIM CLAREY IN WATERCOLOR.

Gadfly — These large flies have a mouth and a single pair of wings that are used for piercing and sucking blood from their victims. They particularly annoy livestock such as horses.

Galaxies — The spiral galaxy that contains our solar system is approximately 100,000 light years in diameter.

Gillyflower — This is the old name for a carnation and is also used to describe plants with fragrant flowers, such as stocks or wallflowers.

Giraffe — These large ruminant animals inhabit the savannahs of tropical Africa. They are the tallest mammals, with long legs and long necks that allow them to eat leaves from trees. Not yet classified as endangered, they are losing their habitat as their homelands are encroached upon by humans.

Glacier — A glacier is a huge, slow-moving mass of ice that originates as an accumulation of snow and then overflows and moves downhill. Glaciers can move at very slow speeds, carving out the landscape as they go.

Glow-worm — These European beetles have luminescent organs that produce a soft greenish light.

Gorilla — The gorilla is the largest of the ape family and lives in the forests of West Africa.

H ILLUSTRATED BY CATHIE FELSTEAD IN WATERCOLOR, INK, OIL COLOR, WAX CRAYON AND BLEACH.

Hare — These solitary mammals are larger than rabbits, with long ears and long legs. They live in shallow nests.

Harebells — A plant with a slender stem and bell-shaped flowers. Also called bluebells.

Hawkmoth — The hawkmoth belongs to a family of moths with long, narrow wings and powerful flight. They can hover over flowers when feeding from the nectar and so are sometimes known as hummingbird hawkmoths.

Honeybee — A social, honey-producing bee that is widely domesticated as a source of honey and beeswax.

Honeybear — This animal is not really a bear, but a tree-dwelling, fruit-eating mammal with a long, prehensile tail. They are members of the raccoon family and are found in Central and South America. The short-tailed ones are known as kinkajou or potto.

I ILLUSTRATED BY DAVID PARKINS IN GOUACHE.

Icebergs — These large masses of polar ice float in the sea, usually broken off from a polar glacier.

J ILLUSTRATED BY KARIN LITTLEWOOD IN WATERCOLOR.

Jasmine — This shrub has fragrant flowers that are used for perfume and also for flavoring tea.

Jaybird — A bird of the crow family, with a pinkish body, blue and black wings, and a black and white crest. They are noisy and quite aggressive birds.

Jellyfish — Found in most oceans and seas, very few are poisonous. They can vary in size from a few inches in diameter to several feet.

Juniper — This coniferous shrub or small tree is found in the northern hemisphere and has purple, berry-like cones.

K ILLUSTRATED BY HELEN WARD IN GOUACHE.

Kingcups — Another name for the Marsh Marigold.

Kingfisher — A beautiful and shy bird with a short tail and sharp bill. They usually live near open water and feed on fish.

L ILLUSTRATED BY JANE RAY IN INK, COLLAGE AND WATERCOLOR.

Lacewing — A pretty, delicate, pale green insect.

Ladybird — An insect traditionally red with black spots, but they actually come in many different colors.

M ILLUSTRATED BY CATHIE FELSTEAD IN WATERCOLOR, INK, OIL COLOR, WAX CRAYON AND BLEACH.

Mammoth — An extinct large, elephant-like mammal with a hairy coat and long, curved tusks. Over the next 100 years, more than half of all the species of animals that have ever lived on earth will have become extinct.

Mayfly — These insects begin life under water, and the fragile, winged adults live briefly in spring, often only for a day.

N ILLUSTRATED BY PATRICK BENSON IN INK LINE ON WATERCOLOR.

Narwhal — The narwhal is an arctic, toothed whale, with a black-spotted whitish skin. The male has a long, spiral tusk. They used to be hunted for their tusks.

Nightingale — A brownish European songbird with a broad, reddish-brown tail, well known for its musical song, usually heard at night.

O ILLUSTRATED BY JANE RAY IN INK, COLLAGE AND WATERCOLOR.

Oak — A common and widespread tree in the United States.

Ocean — More than two thirds of the planet Earth is covered by ocean. There are five oceans in the world, the Atlantic, the Pacific, the Indian, the Arctic and the Antarctic.

P ILLUSTRATED BY JASON COCKROFT IN ACRYLICS.

Planets — As yet, we do not know whether any other planets are capable of supporting life, but there are many planets in the known universe and the chances are that some of them are similar to Earth and so could support life.

Q ILLUSTRATED BY HELEN WARD IN WATERCOLOR AND GOUACHE.

Quagga — This recently extinct member of the horse family looked a little like a zebra, with sandy brown coloring and zebra-like stripes on its head and shoulders. The Quagga Project, a scientific experiment set up in the last few years in Africa, has been attempting to re-create the Quagga through selective breeding of the Plains Zebra, which have the same DNA as the Quagga.

Quaking grass — This is a type of grass found in northern temperate regions and also in South America. It has delicate flower branches that shake in the wind, hence its name.

Quoll — Quolls are the largest carniverous marsupials found on the Australian mainland. They have a red-brown coat marked with white spots, and very sharp teeth. They live on the ground and also in trees, as they are very good climbers. Quoll is the aboriginal name for Tiger Cat, and according to aboriginal legend the white spots on the quoll are spear marks.

R ILLUSTRATED BY CATHIE FELSTEAD IN WATERCOLOR, INK, OIL COLOR, WAX CRAYON AND BLEACH.

Rainbow — Made of the colors of the visible spectrum: red, orange, yellow, green, blue, indigo and violet. After the flood, God placed a rainbow in the sky, as a promise to Noah that he would never again send a flood.

Rainforests — One of the most diverse and complex habitats in the world, supporting a huge number of different life forms, but under threat from commercial development, particularly in South America.

S ILLUSTRATED BY JASON COCKROFT IN ACRYLICS.

Seas — At the moment, the most polluted sea in the world is the North Sea. The Irish Sea is the most radioactive.

Starfish — These are echinoderms, typically with a flattened body and five arms radiating out from a central disc.

Sun — Most people believe all living things on Earth need the sun to survive, if not directly, then because of the beneficial effects of light and warmth from the sun. It is possible we have yet to discover forms of life that do not need the sun.

T ILLUSTRATED BY KARIN LITTLEWOOD IN WATERCOLOR.

Tortoise — Herbivorous reptile of most warm regions,

with heavy, dome-shaped shell and clawed limbs.

Tree — Trees are essential to our survival because they convert carbon dioxide into oxygen. Without trees, the world would be unable to sustain human life.

U ILLUSTRATED BY NICK MALAND IN INK LINE AND WATERCOLOR.

Umbilical cord — The long, flexible tube that feeds the unborn young with oxygen, food, and water. It is vital for survival.

Unborn — Yet to be born; life that is still to come in the future.

Utopias — Imaginary perfect worlds.

V ILLUSTRATED BY TIM CLAREY IN WATERCOLOR.

Vampire Bat — Bat found in tropical regions of Central and Southern America, having sharp incisors and canine teeth. They feed on the blood of birds and mammals.

Violets — A colorful and often fragrant flower that grows wild or in gardens.

Volcanoes — Openings in the earth's crust from which molten lava, rock fragments, ashes, dust and gases are ejected from below the earth's surface.

W ILLUSTRATED BY HELEN WARD IN WATERCOLOR AND INK LINE.

Whale — A large cetacean mammal. Whales have flippers, a streamlined body, and a horizontally flattened tail. They breathe through a blowhole on the top of their heads.

Wolf — Predatory canine mammal that hunts in packs, formerly widespread in North America, Europe and Asia, but now less common.

X ILLUSTRATED BY JASON COCKROFT IN ACRYLICS.

X-Rays — A picture produced by exposing photographic film to radioactivity. They are used in medicine to see things the eye cannot see on its own.

Xeranthemum — Mediterranean plants that have flower heads that are dry and keep their shape and colour for years. Also called Everlasting Flower.

Y ILLUSTRATED BY NICK MALAND IN INK LINE ON WATERCOLOR.

Yeast — Any of various single-celled fungi that reproduce by budding. Yeast is used in bread making and the brewing of beer and whisky. It is an excellent source of B complex vitamins.

Yolk — The substance in an animal ovum that nourishes the growing embryo.

Z ILLUSTRATED BY KARIN LITTLEWOOD IN WATERCOLOR.

Zinnia — Plant of tropical and sub-tropical America with solitary heads of brightly colored flowers. Named after a German botanist who died in 1759.

Zodiac — An imaginary belt that extends 8° on either side of the ecliptic. The zodiac contains the 12 zodiacal constellations, within which the moon and planets appear to move. It is divided into 12 equal areas called the signs of the zodiac.